THE JOY OF
MORE
CLASSICAL MUSIC

T0056417

AMSCO PUBLICATIONS
part of The Music Sales Group

London / New York / Paris / Sydney / Copenhagen / Berlin / Madrid / Tokyo

Published by
Amsco Publications
257 Park Avenue South, New York, NY 10010, USA.

Exclusive Distributors:
Music Sales Corporation
257 Park Avenue South, New York, NY 10010, USA.
Music Sales Limited
14-15 Berners Street, London W1T 3LJ, UK.
Music Sales Pty Limited
20 Resolution Drive, Caringbah, NSW 2229, Australia.

Order No. AM995511
ISBN 978-1-84772-742-8
This book © Copyright 2009 Amsco Publications,
a division of Music Sales Corporation.

Compiled and edited by Sam Harrop.
Cover illustration by Kath Walker.
Printed in the United States of America.

Your Guarantee of Quality
As publishers, we strive to produce every book to the highest commercial standards.
This book has been carefully designed to minimize awkward page turns and to make playing from it a real pleasure.
Particular care has been given to specifying acid-free, neutral-sized paper made from
pulps which have not been elemental chlorine bleached.
This pulp is from farmed sustainable forests and was produced with special regard for the environment.
Throughout, the printing and binding have been planned to ensure a sturdy,
attractive publication which should give years of enjoyment.
If your copy fails to meet our high standards, please inform us and we will gladly replace it.

www.musicsales.com

Piano Sonata No.14 In C# Minor
'Moonlight'

Ludwig van Beethoven

Andantino

FROM PIANO QUINTET IN A MAJOR, OP.114 'TROUT'

Franz Schubert

Andantino

Waltz

FROM 'SWAN LAKE'

Pyotr Il'yich Tchaikovsky

Tempo di valse

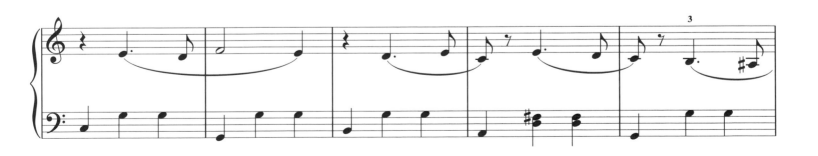

Sarabande In D Minor

George Frideric Handel

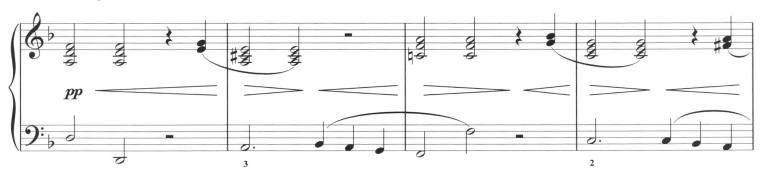

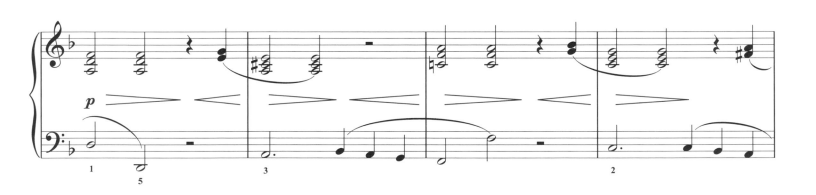

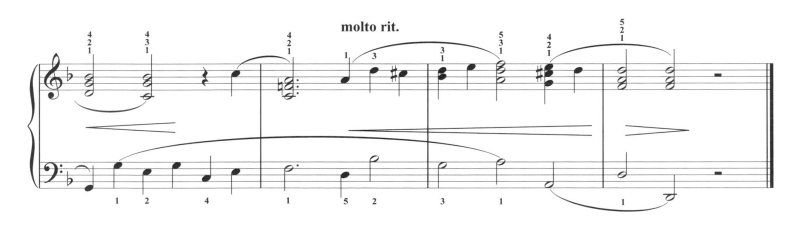

Morning

FROM 'PEER GYNT'

Edvard Grieg

Prelude In E Minor, Op. 28, No. 4

Frédéric Chopin

Songs My Mother Taught Me

Antonín Dvořák

La Charolaise

François Couperin

The Blue Danube

Johann Strauss

Air

FROM ORCHESTRAL SUITE NO. 3 IN D MAJOR 'AIR ON THE G STRING'

Johann Sebastian Bach

Romance In F Major, Op. 50

Ludwig van Beethoven

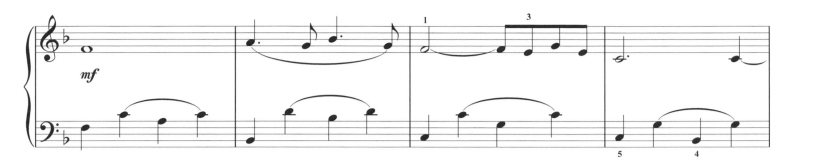

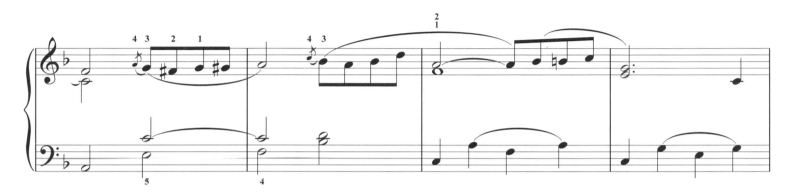

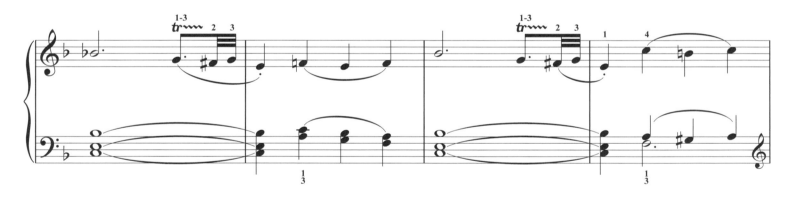

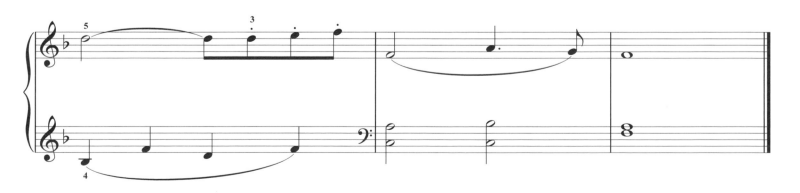

Ave Verum Corpus

Wolfgang Amadeus Mozart

27

Meditation

FROM 'THAÏS'

Jules Massenet

Minuet In G Major

Ludwig van Beethoven

TRIO

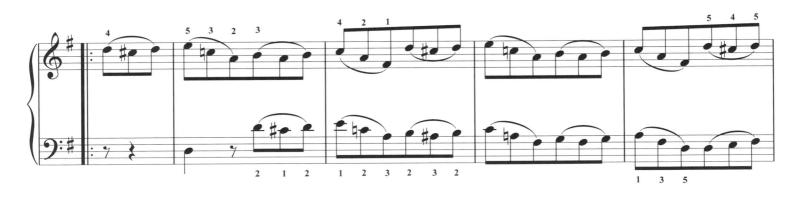

Minuet da capo

31

Pizzicati
FROM 'SYLVIA'
Leo Delibes

Dance Of The Blessed Spirits

FROM 'ORFEO ED EURIDICE'

Christoph Willibald von Gluck

Polonaise In A Major 'Military'

Frédéric Chopin

poco rit.   *D.C. al Fine*

On Wings Of Song

Felix Mendelssohn

* If desired, the original L.H. figuration may be used:

Rondo In D Minor

FROM 'ABDELAZER'

Henry Purcell

Andante

FROM SYMPHONY NO. 6 'PATHÉTIQUE'

Pyotr Il'yich Tchaikovsky

Golliwogg's Cake-Walk

FROM 'CHILDREN'S CORNER'

Claude Debussy

Autumn (3rd Movement)
FROM 'THE FOUR SEASONS'

Antonio Vivaldi

German Dance

Franz Joseph Haydn

Trio

D.C. al Fine

Passepied No.1

Johann Sebastian Bach

(cresc. second time)

1.   **2.**

p

51

Dreaming

Robert Schumann

Largo; Allegro Vivace

FROM FESTIVAL OVERTURE, OP. 49 IN E♭ MAJOR '1812'

Pyotr Il'yich Tchaikovsky

Allegro vivace

Habañera

FROM 'CARMEN'

Georges Bizet

Impromptu In A♭ Major, Op.142, No.2

Franz Schubert

Humoresque

Antonín Dvořák

Étude, Op.10, No.3

Frédéric Chopin

Allegro Vivace

FROM SYMPHONY NO. 41 'JUPITER'

Wolfgang Amadeus Mozart

Overture

FROM 'WILLIAM TELL'

Gioacchino Rossini